FRAPPE
The Ultimate Recipe Book

Les Ilagan

Copyright © CONTENT ARCADE PUBLISHING
All rights reserved.

This cookbook is copyright protected and meant for personal use only. No part of this cookbook may be used, paraphrased, reproduced, scanned, distributed, or sold in any printed or electronic form without permission of the author and the publishing company. Copying pages or any part of this book for any purpose other than own personal use is prohibited and would also mean a violation of copyright law.

DISCLAIMER

Content Arcade Publishing and its authors are joined together in their efforts to create these pages and their publications. Content Arcade Publishing and its authors make no assurance of any kind, stated or implied, with respect to the information provided.

LIMITS OF LIABILITY

Content Arcade Publishing and its authors shall not be held legally responsible in the event of incidental or consequential damages in line with or arising out of, the supplying of the information presented here.

Table of Contents

INTRODUCTION	1
FRAPPE RECIPES	1
BANANA SPLIT FRAPPE	2
CINNAMON-SPICED COFFEE FRAPPE	3
RICH CHOCOLATE FRAPPE	4
CHOCOLATE HAZELNUT FRAPPE	5
ULTIMATE MOCHA FRAPPE	6
CHOCO STRAWBERRY AND COCONUT FRAPPE	7
SOY CHOCOLATE FRAPPE	8
COOKIES AND CREAM FRAPPE	9
DARK MOCHA FRAPPE	10
DECADENT TIRAMISU FRAPPE	11
SUGAR-FREE GREEN TEA FRAPPE	12
HORCHATA FRAPPE	13
MEXICAN CHOCOLATE FRAPPE	14
SPICED PUMPKIN AND CARAMEL FRAPPE	15
CHOCOLATE RASPBERRY FRAPPE	16
WHITE CHOCOLATE FRAPPE	17
CHERRY FRAPPE BLAST	18
COFFEE CARAMEL APPLE FRAPPE	19
COFFEE PEANUT BUTTER FRAPPE	20
CHOCOLATE RICOTTA FRAPPE	21
PEPPERMINT MOCHA FRAPPE	22
ALMOND CHOCOLATE FRAPPE	23
DEEP DARK CHOCOLATE FRAPPE	24
CHOCO BANANA FRAPPE	25
MOCHA JAVA FRAPPE	26
WHITE CHOCOLATE AND CARAMEL FRAPPE	27
ULTIMATE CHOCOLATE AND HAZELNUT FRAPPE	28
STRAWBERRY AND WHITE CHOCOLATE FRAPPE	29
ALMOND CARAMEL COFFEE FRAPPE	30
COFFEE CRUMBLE FRAPPE	31

AMARETTO COFFEE FRAPPE	32
ARABICA COFFEE AND NUTELLA FRAPPE	33
WHITE COFFEE FRAPPE	34
PUMPKIN CARAMEL FRAPPE	35
SPICED MOCHA FRAPPE	36
ALMOND PEACH FRAPPE	37
MACADAMIA CHOCOLATE FRAPPE	38
STRAWBERRY VANILLA FRAPPE	39
CARAMEL MOCHA FRAPPE	40
MINTY MOCHA FRAPPE	41
WHITE MOCHA FRAPPE	42
BLACK FOREST FRAPPE	43
CHERRY VANILLA FRAPPE	44
BANANA AVOCADO FRAPPE	45
LYCHEE AND COCONUT FRAPPE	46
APPLE GREEN TEA FRAPPE	47
TUTTI FRUTTI FRAPPE	48
MANGO BANANA AND ALMOND FRAPPE	49
KIWI COCONUT AND PINEAPPLE FRAPPE	50
BANANA RASPBERRY YOGURT FRAPPE	51
STRAWBERRY BANANA AND YOGURT FRAPPE	52
FRUITY BLAST FRAPPE	53
ULTIMATE CHOCOLATE FRAPPE	54
CHOCO LOCO FRAPPE	55
COOKIE CRUMBLE FRAPPE	56
AVOCADO MATCHA FRAPPE	57
CINNAMON-SPICED APPLE FRAPPE	58
ORANGE PEACH SOY FRAPPE	59
MANGO VANILLA FRAPPE	60
MALTED CHOCO AND BANANA FRAPPE	61
STRAWBERRY KIWI FRAPPE	62
WATERMELON BANANA YOGURT FRAPPE	63
THICK CHOCOLATE FRAPPE WITH MALLOWS	64
MOCHA CHEESECAKE FRAPPE	65
BLUEBERRY BANANA FRAPPE	66

INTRODUCTION

Frappes are cold, blended drinks that are usually made with coffee, chocolate, fruits, milk or dairy, and of course, ice. They are often sold at coffee shops and are loved by millions of people around the world.

This book contains a wide selection of Frappe recipes. So, why don't you surprise your loved ones with a glass of these fine concoctions and for sure they will be delighted!

You can also use your creativity by altering the ingredients to come up with unique frappe recipes. Feel free to mix and match some ingredients to suit your taste. Your options are endless when making this type of blended drinks.

This book is a part of many cookbook series that I am writing; I hope you'll have fun trying all the recipes in this book.

Let's get started!

Frappe Recipes

BANANA SPLIT FRAPPE

Preparation Time	Total Time	Yield
5 minutes	5 minutes	2 servings

INGREDIENTS

- 1 (150 g) frozen banana, peeled and sliced
- 1/2 cup (110 g) frozen strawberries, halved
- 3/4 cup (185 ml) cold milk
- 2 scoops (120 g) chocolate ice cream
- 2 scoops (120 g) vanilla ice cream
- 6 ice cubes
- Whipped cream, to serve
- Chocolate syrup, to serve

METHOD

- Place the banana, strawberries, cold milk, ice cream, and ice cubes in a blender. Then, process until it becomes smooth.
- Pour into 2 chilled tall glasses. Serve topped with some whipped cream and a drizzle of chocolate syrup.
- Enjoy.

NUTRITIONAL INFORMATION

Energy	Fat	Carbohydrates	Protein	Sodium
308 calories	11.5 g	48.3 g	5.8 g	96 mg

CINNAMON-SPICED COFFEE FRAPPE

Preparation Time	Total Time	Yield
5 minutes	5 minutes	2 servings

INGREDIENTS

- 1 cup (250 ml) cooled, strong brewed coffee
- 1/2 cup (125 ml) cold milk
- 2 tablespoons (30 ml) sugar syrup
- 1/2 teaspoon (1 g) ground cinnamon
- 10 ice cubes
- Whipped cream, to serve
- Ground cinnamon, to serve

METHOD

- Place the brewed coffee, cold milk, sugar syrup, cinnamon, and ice cubes in a high-speed blender. Process until smooth.
- Pour into 2 tall glasses. Serve topped with some whipped cream. Sprinkle with more cinnamon.
- Enjoy.

NUTRITIONAL INFORMATION

Energy	Fat	Carbohydrates	Protein	Sodium
230 calories	13.1 g	23.0 g	7.0 g	108 mg

RICH CHOCOLATE FRAPPE

Preparation Time	Total Time	Yield
5 minutes	5 minutes	2 servings

INGREDIENTS

- 2 tablespoons (15 g) cocoa powder, unsweetened
- 1/4 cup (60 ml) hot water
- 1/3 cup (120 ml) chocolate syrup
- 1 ½ cups (375 ml) cold milk
- 10-12 ice cubes
- Chocolate ice cream, to serve (optional)

METHOD

- Combine the cocoa powder and hot water in a cup; stir until dissolved completely. Pour into a blender.
- Add the chocolate syrup, vanilla extract, milk, and ice cubes. Blend until smooth.
- Pour into 2 chilled tall glasses. Top with chocolate ice cream, if desired.
- Serve and enjoy.

NUTRITIONAL INFORMATION

Energy	Fat	Carbohydrates	Protein	Sodium
281 calories	7.3 g	49.5 g	7.3 g	122 mg

CHOCOLATE HAZELNUT FRAPPE

Preparation Time	Total Time	Yield
5 minutes	5 minutes	2 servings

INGREDIENTS

- 2 scoops (120 g) chocolate ice cream
- 2 tablespoons (30 ml) hazelnut syrup
- 1 cup (250 ml) cold milk
- 8 ice cubes
- Whipped cream, to serve
- Chocolate shavings, to serve
- Vanilla wafer rolls, to serve

METHOD

- Combine the chocolate ice cream, hazelnut syrup, milk, and ice cubes in a blender. Process until smooth.
- Pour into 2 chilled glasses. Serve topped with some whipped cream, chocolate shavings, and wafer rolls.
- Enjoy.

NUTRITIONAL INFORMATION

Energy	Fat	Carbohydrates	Protein	Sodium
325 calories	19.8 g	29.6 g	8.1 g	132 mg

ULTIMATE MOCHA FRAPPE

Preparation Time	Total Time	Yield
5 minutes	5 minutes	2 servings

INGREDIENTS

- 3 shots (90 ml) espresso
- 1/3 cup (100 ml) chocolate syrup
- 1 cup (250 ml) whole milk
- 8-10 ice cubes
- Whipped cream, to serve
- Chocolate shavings, to serve

METHOD

- Combine espresso, chocolate syrup, milk, and ice cubes in a blender. Process until smooth.
- Pour into 2 chilled glasses. Serve topped with some whipped cream and chocolate shavings.
- Enjoy.

NUTRITIONAL INFORMATION

Energy	Fat	Carbohydrates	Protein	Sodium
272 calories	12.0 g	35.7 g	5.6 g	96 mg

CHOCO STRAWBERRY AND COCONUT FRAPPE

Preparation Time	Total Time	Yield
5 minutes	5 minutes	2 servings

INGREDIENTS

- 1 cup (220 g) frozen strawberries, hulled and halved
- 1/4 cup (60 ml) coconut milk
- 1/4 cup (80 ml) chocolate syrup
- 3/4 cup (185 ml) cold skim milk
- 8 ice cubes
- Fresh mint, for garnish

METHOD

- In a blender, combine the strawberries, coconut milk, chocolate syrup, skim milk, and ice cubes. Process until smooth.
- Pour into 2 chilled glasses. Garnish with fresh mint.
- Serve and enjoy.

NUTRITIONAL INFORMATION

Energy	Fat	Carbohydrates	Protein	Sodium
247 calories	10.1 g	35.3 g	5.5 g	89 mg

SOY CHOCOLATE FRAPPE

Preparation Time	Total Time	Yield
5 minutes	5 minutes	2 servings

INGREDIENTS

- 6 oz. (185 g) silken tofu
- 1 ½ cups (375 ml) chocolate flavored soy milk
- 2 tablespoons (40 ml) chocolate syrup
- 8 ice cubes
- Whipped cream, to serve
- Chocolate candy sprinkles, to serve

METHOD

- Combine the tofu, soy milk, chocolate syrup, and ice cubes in a blender. Process until smooth.
- Pour into 2 chilled tall glasses. Serve topped with some whipped cream. Sprinkle with chocolate candy sprinkles.
- Enjoy.

NUTRITIONAL INFORMATION

Energy	Fat	Carbohydrates	Protein	Sodium
255 calories	6.4 g	40.0 g	8.1 g	105 mg

COOKIES AND CREAM FRAPPE

Preparation Time	Total Time	Yield
5 minutes	5 minutes	2 servings

INGREDIENTS

- 1 ½ cups cold skim milk
- 4 (12 g) Oreo cookies, crushed
- 2 scoops (120 g) chocolate-flavored ice cream
- 2 tablespoons (40 ml) chocolate syrup
- 8 ice cubes
- 2 (12 g) whole Oreo cookies, for garnish
- Whipped cream, to serve
- Crushed Oreo cookies, to serve

METHOD

- In a blender, combine the milk, crushed Oreo cookies, ice cream, chocolate syrup, and ice cubes. Process until smooth
- Pour frappe into 2 chilled tall glasses.
- Top with some whipped cream and garnish with crushed and whole Oreo cookies.
- Serve and enjoy.

NUTRITIONAL INFORMATION

Energy	Fat	Carbohydrates	Protein	Sodium
380 calories	17.2 g	47.0 g	10.9 g	257 mg

DARK MOCHA FRAPPE

Preparation Time	Total Time	Yield
5 minutes	5 minutes	2 servings

INGREDIENTS

- 1 ½ cups (375 ml) strong brewed coffee, cooled
- 1/3 cup (100 ml) dark chocolate syrup
- 8-10 milk ice cubes
- Whipped cream, to serve

METHOD

- Put the brewed coffee, milk ice cubes, and dark chocolate syrup in a blender; blend until smooth.
- Pour into 2 chilled glasses. Top with some whipped cream and drizzle with more chocolate syrup if desired.
- Serve and enjoy.

NUTRITIONAL INFORMATION

Energy	Fat	Carbohydrates	Protein	Sodium
223 calories	8.6 g	32.9 g	5.3 g	92 mg

DECADENT TIRAMISU FRAPPE

Preparation Time	Total Time	Yield
5 minutes	5 minutes	2 servings

INGREDIENTS

- 2 tablespoons (15 g) unsweetened cocoa powder
- 2 tablespoons (30 ml) hot water
- 1 ½ cups (375 ml) cold almond milk
- 1/3 cup (85 g) cream cheese
- 1/2 cup (125 ml) strong brewed coffee, cooled
- 1/4 cup (80 ml) chocolate syrup
- 1/4 teaspoon (1 ml) vanilla extract
- 1/4 teaspoon (1 ml) orange extract
- 8-10 ice cubes
- Whipped cream, to serve
- Cocoa powder, for garnish

METHOD

- In a small bowl, dissolve cocoa powder in hot water. Then pour mixture in a blender.
- Add in the almond milk, cream cheese, brewed coffee, chocolate syrup, vanilla extract, orange extract, and ice cubes. Process until smooth.
- Pour into 2 chilled glasses. Serve topped with some whipped cream and sprinkle with cocoa powder.
- Enjoy.

NUTRITIONAL INFORMATION

Energy	Fat	Carbohydrates	Protein	Sodium
273 calories	16.8 g	27.7 g	4.4 g	195 mg

SUGAR-FREE GREEN TEA FRAPPE

Preparation Time	Total Time	Yield
5 minutes	5 minutes	2 servings

INGREDIENTS

- 1 ½ cups (375 ml) cold milk
- 1 tablespoon (7 g) green tea powder or matcha
- 1/4 teaspoon (1.5 ml) vanilla extract
- 10 ice cubes
- Liquid Stevia, to taste
- Whipped cream, to serve
- Green tea powder, for garnish

METHOD

- Combine the milk, green tea powder, and vanilla in a blender. Pulse a few times to dissolve the green tea powder.
- Then add the ice cubes and process to your desired consistency.
- Add 2-3 drops of liquid Stevia to taste.
- Pour into 2 chilled glasses. Top with some whipped cream and sprinkle with green tea powder.
- Serve and enjoy.

NUTRITIONAL INFORMATION

Energy	Fat	Carbohydrates	Protein	Sodium
140 calories	8.4 g	9.5 g	7.3 g	91 mg

HORCHATA FRAPPE

Preparation Time	Total Time	Yield
5 minutes	15 minutes	3 servings

INGREDIENTS

- 2 cups (500 ml) water
- 1 cinnamon stick
- 1 star anise seed
- 1/8 teaspoon nutmeg
- 1/8 teaspoon cardamom, ground
- 3 (2 g) black tea bags
- 3 tablespoons (45 g) brown sugar
- 15 milk ice cubes
- Whipped cream, to serve
- Ground cinnamon, to serve

METHOD

- In a pot or saucepan, bring water to a boil and add the cinnamon, star anise, nutmeg, and cardamom. Cook for 3 minutes.
- Add the tea bags in the spiced water and steep for about 5 minutes. Take out and discard the tea bags and allow to cool.
- Combine the cooled tea and sugar in a blender along with the milk ice cubes. Blend together until smooth.
- Pour into 3 chilled glasses. Serve topped with some whipped cream and sprinkle with ground cinnamon.
- Serve immediately and enjoy.

NUTRITIONAL INFORMATION

Energy	Fat	Carbohydrates	Protein	Sodium
136 calories	3.4 g	21.7 g	5.7 g	82 mg

MEXICAN CHOCOLATE FRAPPE

Preparation Time	Total Time	Yield
5 minutes	5 minutes	2 servings

INGREDIENTS

- 1 cup (250 ml) milk
- 1/4 cup (80 g) Mexican chocolate, melted
- 1 tablespoon (15 g) brown sugar
- 8-10 ice cubes
- Whipped cream, to serve
- Chocolate syrup, to serve

METHOD

- Blend the milk, Mexican chocolate, and brown sugar in a blender. Pulse to mix the ingredients. Add the ice cubes, and then process until smooth.
- Pour into 2 chilled glasses. Serve topped with some whipped cream and drizzle with chocolate syrup.
- Serve and enjoy.

NUTRITIONAL INFORMATION

Energy	Fat	Carbohydrates	Protein	Sodium
265 calories	10.5 g	40.1 g	5.5 g	82 mg

SPICED PUMPKIN AND CARAMEL FRAPPE

Preparation Time	Total Time	Yield
5 minutes	5 minutes	2 servings

INGREDIENTS

- 1 cup (250 ml) cold milk
- 1/2 cup (125 ml) strong brewed coffee, cooled
- 1/2 cup (125 g) pumpkin puree
- 1/2 teaspoon (1 g) pumpkin spice
- 3 tablespoons (60 g) caramel sauce
- 10-12 ice cubes
- Whipped cream, to serve
- Caramel sauce, to serve

METHOD

- Pulse the milk, brewed coffee, pumpkin puree, pumpkin spice, and caramel sauce in a blender until combined well. Add the ice cubes and then process until smooth.
- Pour into 2 tall chilled glasses. Top with some whipped cream and drizzle with caramel sauce.
- Serve and enjoy.

NUTRITIONAL INFORMATION

Energy	Fat	Carbohydrates	Protein	Sodium
161 calories	2.8 g	31.5 g	5.2 g	169 mg

CHOCOLATE RASPBERRY FRAPPE

Preparation Time	Total Time	Yield
5 minutes	5 minutes	2 servings

INGREDIENTS

- 1 cup (250 ml) whole milk
- 3/4 cup (95 g) fresh raspberries
- 1/4 cup (80 ml) dark chocolate, melted
- 2 tablespoons (30 g) brown sugar
- 1 tablespoon (7 g) cocoa powder
- 1/4 teaspoon (1.5 ml) vanilla extract
- 8-10 ice cubes
- Chocolate syrup, to serve
- Chocolate ice cream, to serve (optional)

METHOD

- Place the milk, raspberries, melted dark chocolate, brown sugar, cocoa powder, and vanilla in a blender. Pulse 2-3 times to combine.
- Add the ice cubes and then process until smooth.
- Drizzle some chocolate syrup in 2 chilled glasses to decorate the sides then pour the blended frappe. Top with a scoop of chocolate ice cream, if desired.
- Serve and enjoy.

NUTRITIONAL INFORMATION

Energy	Fat	Carbohydrates	Protein	Sodium
264 calories	10.6 g	37.4 g	6.3 g	66 mg

WHITE CHOCOLATE FRAPPE

Preparation Time	Total Time	Yield
5 minutes	5 minutes	2 servings

INGREDIENTS

- 1 cup (250 ml) almond milk, unsweetened
- 3 oz. (85 g) white chocolate, melted
- 3 oz. (85 g) vanilla ice cream
- 8-10 ice cubes
- Whipped cream, to serve
- Crumbled chocolate cookies, to serve

METHOD

- Combine the almond milk and white chocolate in a blender. Pulse until blended well.
- Add the vanilla ice cream and ice cubes. Process until smooth.
- Pour into 2 chilled glasses. Top with some whipped cream and crumbled chocolate cookies.
- Serve and enjoy.

NUTRITIONAL INFORMATION

Energy	Fat	Carbohydrates	Protein	Sodium
302 calories	17.9 g	32.5 g	7.3 g	153 mg

CHERRY FRAPPE BLAST

Preparation Time	Total Time	Yield
5 minutes	5 minutes	2 servings

INGREDIENTS

- 2 scoops (120 g) vanilla ice cream
- 1 cup (250 ml) cold milk
- 1/2 cup (75 g) pitted sweet cherries
- 10-12 ice cubes
- 2 halves maraschino cherry, to serve
- Whipped cream, to serve
- Candy sprinkles, to serve
- Cherry syrup, to serve

METHOD

- Combine the vanilla ice cream, cold milk, sweet cherries, and ice cubes in a blender. Process until smooth.
- Pour into 2 chilled glasses. Top with some whipped cream, maraschino cherry, and candy sprinkles. Finally, drizzle with cherry syrup.
- Serve and enjoy.

NUTRITIONAL INFORMATION

Energy	Fat	Carbohydrates	Protein	Sodium
269 calories	14.2 g	29.0 g	7.0 g	121 mg

COFFEE CARAMEL APPLE FRAPPE

Preparation Time	Total Time	Yield
5 minutes	5 minutes	1 servings

INGREDIENTS

- 1 shot (30 ml) espresso
- 1/2 cup (125 ml) milk
- 2 tablespoons (30 g) apple sauce
- 2 tablespoons (40 ml) caramel sauce
- 1 tablespoon (15 ml) apple juice concentrate
- 6 ice cubes
- Whipped cream, to serve

METHOD

- Combine the espresso, milk, applesauce, caramel sauce, apple juice concentrate, and ice cubes in a high-speed blender. Process until smooth.
- Pour into a chilled glass. Top with some whipped cream or ice cream and then drizzle with caramel sauce if desired.
- Serve and enjoy.

NUTRITIONAL INFORMATION

Energy	Fat	Carbohydrates	Protein	Sodium
290 calories	11.8 g	43.5 g	5.4 g	215 mg

COFFEE PEANUT BUTTER FRAPPE

Preparation Time	Total Time	Yield
5 minutes	5 minutes	1 servings

INGREDIENTS

- 1 shot (30 ml) espresso
- 1/2 cup (125 ml) milk
- 2 tablespoons (40 g) peanut butter
- 2 tablespoons (40 g) caramel sauce
- 6 ice cubes
- Whipped cream, to serve (optional)
- Chopped dry roasted peanuts, to serve (optional)

METHOD

- Combine the espresso, milk, peanut butter, caramel sauce, and ice cubes in a high-speed blender. Process until smooth.
- Pour into a chilled glass. Top with some whipped cream, and chopped peanuts. Drizzle with caramel sauce if desired.
- Serve and enjoy.

NUTRITIONAL INFORMATION

Energy	Fat	Carbohydrates	Protein	Sodium
357 calories	18.6 g	40.3 g	12.6 g	355 mg

CHOCOLATE RICOTTA FRAPPE

Preparation Time	Total Time	Yield
5 minutes	5 minutes	2 servings

INGREDIENTS

- 1 1/2 cups (375 ml) chocolate flavored milk
- 1/4 cup (60 g) ricotta cheese
- 12 ice cubes
- 2 tablespoons (40 ml) thick chocolate syrup
- Whipped cream, to serve
- Chocolate chips, to serve
- Fresh mint, for garnish

METHOD

- Combine the chocolate flavored milk, ricotta cheese, and ice cubes in a high speed blender. Blend until smooth.
- Drizzle some chocolate syrup at the bottom of a tall glass and then pour the chocolate frappe.
- Top with some whipped cream, chocolate chips, and mint.
- Serve and enjoy.

NUTRITIONAL INFORMATION

Energy	Fat	Carbohydrates	Protein	Sodium
339 calories	15.3 g	41.6 g	11.1 g	183 mg

PEPPERMINT MOCHA FRAPPE

Preparation Time	Total Time	Yield
5 minutes	5 minutes	2 servings

INGREDIENTS

- 3 shots (90 ml) espresso
- 1 cup (250 ml) milk
- 2 tablespoons (40 ml) chocolate syrup
- 1 tablespoon (15 ml) peppermint syrup
- 12 ice cubes
- Fresh peppermint, for garnish

METHOD

- Combine the espresso, milk, chocolate syrup, peppermint syrup, and ice cubes in a high-speed blender. Process until smooth.
- Pour into 2 chilled glass. Garnish with mint sprig.
- Serve and enjoy.

NUTRITIONAL INFORMATION

Energy	Fat	Carbohydrates	Protein	Sodium
271 calories	3.8 g	53.4 g	6.1 g	111 mg

ALMOND CHOCOLATE FRAPPE

Preparation Time	Total Time	Yield
5 minutes	5 minutes	2 servings

INGREDIENTS

- 1 cup (250 ml) almond milk, unsweetened
- 2 scoops (120 g) chocolate ice cream
- 2 tablespoons (40 ml) chocolate syrup
- 1/2 teaspoon (2.5 ml) almond extract
- 8-10 ice cubes
- Chocolate chips, to serve
- Whipped cream, to serve

METHOD

- Combine the almond milk, chocolate ice cream, chocolate syrup, almond extract, and ice cubes in a high-speed blender.
- Pour into 2 chilled glasses. Serve topped with whipped cream and some chocolate chips.
- Enjoy.

NUTRITIONAL INFORMATION

Energy	Fat	Carbohydrates	Protein	Sodium
279 calories	14.7 g	32.4 g	3.9 g	154 mg

DEEP DARK CHOCOLATE FRAPPE

Preparation Time	Total Time	Yield
5 minutes	5 minutes	2 servings

INGREDIENTS

- 1 cup (250 ml) milk
- 2 scoops (120 g) chocolate ice cream
- 1/4 cup (80 ml) dark chocolate sauce
- 8 ice cubes
- Whipped cream, to serve
- Chocolate syrup, to serve

METHOD

- In a blender, combine the milk, chocolate ice cream, dark chocolate sauce, and ice cubes. Blend until smooth.
- Pour into 2 chilled glasses. Serve topped with some whipped cream and drizzle with chocolate syrup.
- Enjoy.

NUTRITIONAL INFORMATION

Energy	Fat	Carbohydrates	Protein	Sodium
330 calories	12.1 g	46.9 g	7.4 g	154 mg

CHOCO BANANA FRAPPE

Preparation Time	Total Time	Yield
5 minutes	5 minutes	2 servings

INGREDIENTS

- 1 (180 g) frozen banana, cut into small pieces
- 1 cup (250 ml) milk
- 2 scoops (120 g) chocolate ice cream
- 8 ice cubes
- Whipped cream, to serve
- Chocolate syrup, to serve

METHOD

- In a blender, combine the banana, milk, chocolate ice cream, and ice cubes. Blend until smooth.
- Pour into 2 chilled glasses. Serve topped with some whipped cream. Drizzle with chocolate syrup.
- Enjoy.

NUTRITIONAL INFORMATION

Energy	Fat	Carbohydrates	Protein	Sodium
347 calories	14.5 g	48.1 g	7.7 g	133 mg

MOCHA JAVA FRAPPE

Preparation Time	Total Time	Yield
5 minutes	5 minutes	2 servings

INGREDIENTS

- 2 scoops (120 g) coffee-flavored ice cream
- 1 shot (30 ml) espresso
- 1 cup (250 ml) milk
- 1 tablespoon (7 g) cocoa powder
- 1/4 teaspoon (0.5 g) cinnamon, ground
- 1/4 teaspoon (0.5 g) nutmeg, ground
- 8 ice cubes
- Whipped cream, to serve
- Chocolate syrup, to serve

METHOD

- In a blender, combine the ice cream, espresso, milk, cocoa powder, cinnamon, nutmeg, and ice cubes. Blend until smooth.
- Pour into 2 chilled tall glasses. Serve topped with whipped cream and drizzle with chocolate syrup.
- Enjoy.

NUTRITIONAL INFORMATION

Energy	Fat	Carbohydrates	Protein	Sodium
307 calories	14.8 g	37.5 g	7.6 g	134 mg

WHITE CHOCOLATE AND CARAMEL FRAPPE

Preparation Time	Total Time	Yield
5 minutes	5 minutes	2 servings

INGREDIENTS

- 2 tablespoons (40 ml) white chocolate syrup
- 2 tablespoons (40 ml) caramel syrup
- 2 scoops (120 g) vanilla ice cream
- 1 cup (250 ml) skim milk
- 8 ice cubes
- Whipped cream, to serve
- Caramel syrup, to serve

METHOD

- In a blender, combine the white chocolate syrup, caramel syrup, vanilla ice cream, milk, and ice cubes. Blend until smooth and creamy.
- Pour into 2 chilled glasses. Serve topped with some whipped cream and drizzle with caramel syrup.
- Enjoy.

NUTRITIONAL INFORMATION

Energy	Fat	Carbohydrates	Protein	Sodium
336 calories	10.9 g	53.7 g	6.9 g	233 mg

ULTIMATE CHOCOLATE AND HAZELNUT FRAPPE

Preparation Time	Total Time	Yield
5 minutes	5 minutes	2 servings

INGREDIENTS

- 2 tablespoons (40 ml) hazelnut syrup
- 2 scoops (120 g) chocolate ice cream
- 1/4 teaspoon (1.5 ml) vanilla extract
- 1 cup (250 ml) almond milk, unsweetened
- 8 ice cubes
- Whipped cream, to serve
- Chocolate syrup, to serve

METHOD

- Put the hazelnut syrup, chocolate ice cream, vanilla extract, almond milk, and ice cubes in a high-speed blender. Blend until smooth.
- Pour into 2 chilled glasses. Serve topped with some whipped cream. Drizzle with chocolate syrup.
- Enjoy.

NUTRITIONAL INFORMATION

Energy	Fat	Carbohydrates	Protein	Sodium
245 calories	14.2 g	26.0 g	3.7 g	133 mg

STRAWBERRY AND WHITE CHOCOLATE FRAPPE

Preparation Time	Total Time	Yield
5 minutes	5 minutes	2 servings

INGREDIENTS

- 2 scoops (120 g) strawberry ice cream
- 2 tablespoons (40 ml) white chocolate syrup
- 1 cup (250 ml) milk
- 8 ice cubes
- Whipped cream, to serve

METHOD

- Combine the strawberry ice cream, white chocolate syrup, milk, and ice cubes in a blender. Process until smooth.
- Pour the frappe into 2 chilled glasses. Serve topped with some whipped cream.
- Enjoy.

NUTRITIONAL INFORMATION

Energy	Fat	Carbohydrates	Protein	Sodium
294 calories	14.4 g	34.7 g	7.0 g	133 mg

ALMOND CARAMEL COFFEE FRAPPE

Preparation Time	Total Time	Yield
5 minutes	5 minutes	2 servings

INGREDIENTS

- 1/4 cup (80 g) caramel sauce
- 1/4 teaspoon (1.5 ml) vanilla extract
- 3 shots (90 ml) espresso
- 1 cup (250 ml) almond milk, unsweetened
- 10-12 ice cubes

METHOD

- In a blender, combine the caramel sauce, vanilla extract, espresso, almond milk, and ice cubes. Blend until smooth.
- Pour into 2 chilled glasses.
- Serve and enjoy.

NUTRITIONAL INFORMATION

Energy	Fat	Carbohydrates	Protein	Sodium
189 calories	2.6 g	39.0 g	4.8 g	232 mg

COFFEE CRUMBLE FRAPPE

Preparation Time	Total Time	Yield
5 minutes	5 minutes	2 servings

INGREDIENTS

- 3 shots (90 ml) espresso
- 3 scoops (180 g) vanilla ice cream
- 1 cup (250 ml) almond milk, unsweetened
- 3 (12 g) Oreo cookies, crushed
- 2 tablespoons (40 ml) chocolate syrup
- 2 tablespoons (15 g) dry roasted cashew nuts
- 8-10 ice cubes
- Fresh mint sprigs, for garnish
- Coffee beans, for garnish

METHOD

- Combine the espresso, vanilla ice cream, almond milk, Oreo cookies, chocolate syrup, cashew nuts, and ice cubes in a blender. Process until smooth.
- Pour into 2 chilled glasses. Garnish with mint sprigs and some coffee beans.
- Serve and enjoy.

NUTRITIONAL INFORMATION

Energy	Fat	Carbohydrates	Protein	Sodium
310 calories	14.6 g	40.7 g	5.1 g	210 mg

AMARETTO COFFEE FRAPPE

Preparation Time	Total Time	Yield
5 minutes	5 minutes	2 servings

INGREDIENTS

- 1 cup (250 ml) very strong brewed coffee, cooled
- 2 scoops (120 g) vanilla ice cream
- 2 tablespoons (30 ml) amaretto liqueur
- 2 tablespoons (40 ml) melted dark chocolate
- 1 cup (250 ml) skim milk
- 10 ice cubes
- Whipped cream, to serve

METHOD

- Combine the brewed coffee, ice cream, amaretto, chocolate syrup, milk, and ice cubes in a blender. Blend until smooth.
- Pour into 2 chilled glasses. Serve topped with some whipped cream.
- Enjoy.

NUTRITIONAL INFORMATION

Energy	Fat	Carbohydrates	Protein	Sodium
292 calories	14.6 g	22.7 g	6.6 g	174 mg

ARABICA COFFEE AND NUTELLA FRAPPE

Preparation Time	Total Time	Yield
5 minutes	5 minutes	2 servings

INGREDIENTS

- 1 cup (250 ml) strong Arabica coffee, cooled
- 1 cup (250 g) vanilla ice cream
- 1/2 cup (125 ml) milk
- 2 tablespoons (40 g) Nutella Hazelnut Spread with Cocoa
- 8 ice cubes
- Ground cinnamon, to serve

METHOD

- In a blender, combine the Arabica coffee, vanilla ice cream, milk, Nutella, and ice cubes. Blend until smooth.
- Pour into 2 chilled glasses. Sprinkle with some ground cinnamon.
- Serve and enjoy.

NUTRITIONAL INFORMATION

Energy	Fat	Carbohydrates	Protein	Sodium
312 calories	16.0 g	35.6 g	6.1 g	105 mg

WHITE COFFEE FRAPPE

Preparation Time	Total Time	Yield
5 minutes	5 minutes	1 servings

INGREDIENTS

- 1 shot (30 ml) espresso
- 1 scoop (60 g) vanilla ice cream
- 6 ice cubes
- 3/4 cup (185 ml) skim milk
- Whipped cream, to serve
- Chocolate syrup, to serve

METHOD

- Combine the espresso, vanilla ice cream, ice cubes, and milk in a blender. Process until smooth.
- Pour into a chilled glass. Serve topped with some whipped cream. Drizzle with chocolate syrup.
- Enjoy.

NUTRITIONAL INFORMATION

Energy	Fat	Carbohydrates	Protein	Sodium
298 calories	12.8 g	35.2 g	7.0 g	120 mg

PUMPKIN CARAMEL FRAPPE

Preparation Time	Total Time	Yield
5 minutes	5 minutes	2 servings

INGREDIENTS

- 1 cup (250 ml) strong brewed coffee
- 1/2 cup (125 g) pumpkin puree
- 1/4 cup (80 ml) caramel sauce
- 1/4 teaspoon (1 g) pumpkin pie spice
- 1 cup (250 ml) cold milk
- 12 ice cubes

METHOD

- Combine the brewed coffee, pumpkin puree, caramel sauce, pumpkin pie spice, cold milk, and ice cubes together in a high-speed blender. Process until smooth.
- Pour into 2 chilled glasses. Drizzle with caramel syrup.
- Serve and enjoy.

NUTRITIONAL INFORMATION

Energy	Fat	Carbohydrates	Protein	Sodium
180 calories	2.7 g	35.1 g	4.8 g	68 mg

SPICED MOCHA FRAPPE

Preparation Time	Total Time	Yield
5 minutes	5 minutes	2 servings

INGREDIENTS

- 1 cup (250 ml) strong brewed coffee
- 1 tablespoon (7 g) cocoa powder
- 2 tablespoons (40 ml) sweetened condensed milk
- 2 tablespoons (40 ml) chocolate syrup
- 1/4 teaspoon (0.5 g) ground cinnamon
- 1/4 teaspoon (0.5 g) nutmeg
- 3/4 cup (185 ml) cold milk
- 10-12 ice cubes
- Whipped cream, to serve

METHOD

- In a blender, combine the coffee, cocoa powder, condensed milk, cinnamon, nutmeg, milk, and ice cubes. Blend until smooth.
- Pour into 2 chilled glasses. Serve topped with some whipped cream.
- Serve and enjoy.

NUTRITIONAL INFORMATION

Energy	Fat	Carbohydrates	Protein	Sodium
245 calories	6.5 g	40.8 g	8.1 g	126 mg

ALMOND PEACH FRAPPE

Preparation Time	Total Time	Yield
5 minutes	5 minutes	2 servings

INGREDIENTS

- 3 peach halves (225 g), cut into small pieces
- 3 scoops (180 g) vanilla ice cream
- 1 cup (250 ml) almond milk, unsweetened
- 8 ice cubes
- Caramel syrup, to serve

METHOD

- Place the peaches, ice cream, almond milk, and ice cubes in a blender. Process until smooth.
- Pour into 2 chilled glasses. Drizzle with some caramel syrup.
- Serve immediately and enjoy.

NUTRITIONAL INFORMATION

Energy	Fat	Carbohydrates	Protein	Sodium
205 calories	8.0 g	30.7 g	4.2 g	123 mg

MACADAMIA CHOCOLATE FRAPPE

Preparation Time	Total Time	Yield
5 minutes	5 minutes	2 servings

INGREDIENTS

- 3 scoops (180 g) chocolate ice cream
- 2 tablespoons (30 ml) macadamia syrup
- 1 cup (250 ml) milk
- 8 ice cubes
- Whipped cream, to serve
- Cocoa powder, to serve

METHOD

- Combine the ice cream, macadamia syrup, milk, and ice cubes in a high-speed blender. Process until smooth.
- Pour into 2 chilled glasses. Serve topped with whipped cream. Sprinkle with some cocoa powder.
- Serve immediately and enjoy.

NUTRITIONAL INFORMATION

Energy	Fat	Carbohydrates	Protein	Sodium
254 calories	16.0 g	22.1 g	6.9 g	114 mg

STRAWBERRY VANILLA FRAPPE

Preparation Time	Total Time	Yield
5 minutes	5 minutes	2 servings

INGREDIENTS

- 1 cup (220 g) frozen strawberries
- 1 cup (250 ml) cold milk
- 2 scoops (120 g) vanilla ice cream
- 2 tablespoons (30 ml) strawberry syrup

METHOD

- In a blender, combine the strawberries, milk, ice cream, and strawberry syrup. Blend until smooth.
- Pour into 2 chilled glasses.
- Serve and enjoy.

NUTRITIONAL INFORMATION

Energy	Fat	Carbohydrates	Protein	Sodium
228 calories	9.5 g	44.8 g	6.3 g	111 mg

CARAMEL MOCHA FRAPPE

Preparation Time	Total Time	Yield
5 minutes	5 minutes	2 servings

INGREDIENTS

- 3 shots (90 ml) espresso
- 1/4 cup (80 g) caramel sauce
- 1 tablespoon (7 g) cocoa powder, dissolved in 2 tablespoons hot water
- 1 cup (250 ml) cold milk
- 12 ice cubes
- Whipped cream, to serve
- Chocolate syrup, to serve

METHOD

- In a blender, combine the espresso, caramel sauce, cocoa, milk, and ice cubes. Process until smooth.
- Pour into 2 chilled glasses. Serve topped with whipped cream. Drizzle with chocolate syrup. Garnish with fresh strawberry, if desired.
- Enjoy.

NUTRITIONAL INFORMATION

Energy	Fat	Carbohydrates	Protein	Sodium
288 calories	10.1 g	45.1 g	6.2 g	220 mg

MINTY MOCHA FRAPPE

Preparation Time	Total Time	Yield
5 minutes	5 minutes	2 servings

INGREDIENTS

- 3 shots (90 ml) espresso
- 1 tablespoon (7 g) cocoa powder, dissolved in 2 tablespoons hot water
- 2 tablespoons (40 ml) chocolate syrup
- 2 tablespoons (30 ml) peppermint syrup
- 1 cup (250 ml) cold milk
- 12 ice cubes
- Whipped cream, to serve
- Chocolate syrup, to serve

METHOD

- In a blender, combine the espresso, cocoa, peppermint syrup, cold milk, and ice cubes. Blend until smooth.
- Pour into 2 chilled glasses. Serve frappe topped with some whipped cream and a drizzle of chocolate syrup.
- Enjoy.

NUTRITIONAL INFORMATION

Energy	Fat	Carbohydrates	Protein	Sodium
258 calories	10.2 g	35.3 g	5.8 g	93 mg

WHITE MOCHA FRAPPE

Preparation Time	Total Time	Yield
5 minutes	5 minutes	2 servings

INGREDIENTS

- 2 shots (60 ml) espresso
- 2 scoops (120 g) vanilla ice cream
- 3 tablespoons (60 ml) white chocolate sauce
- 1 cup (250 ml) milk
- 12 ice cubes
- Whipped cream, to serve
- Chocolate syrup, to serve

METHOD

- Combine espresso, vanilla ice cream, white chocolate sauce, milk, and ice cubes. Process until smooth.
- Pour into 2 chilled glasses. Serve topped with some whipped cream and drizzle with chocolate syrup.
- Enjoy.

NUTRITIONAL INFORMATION

Energy	Fat	Carbohydrates	Protein	Sodium
353 calories	15.8 g	48.6 g	6.8 g	181 mg

BLACK FOREST FRAPPE

Preparation Time	Total Time	Yield
5 minutes	5 minutes	2 servings

INGREDIENTS

- 1 cup (250 ml) milk
- 1 cup (250 g) chocolate ice cream
- 12 ice cubes
- 2 tablespoons (30 ml) cherry syrup
- 1/4 teaspoon (1.5 ml) vanilla extract
- Maraschino cherries, to serve
- Whipped cream, to serve
- Chocolate syrup, to serve

METHOD

- Combine the milk, chocolate ice cream, ice cubes, cherry syrup, and vanilla extract in a blender. Process until smooth.
- Pour into 2 chilled tall glasses. Serve topped with whipped cream and cherry. Drizzle with chocolate syrup.
- Enjoy.

NUTRITIONAL INFORMATION

Energy	Fat	Carbohydrates	Protein	Sodium
345 calories	14.3 g	46.6 g	6.8 g	141 mg

CHERRY VANILLA FRAPPE

Preparation Time	Total Time	Yield
5 minutes	5 minutes	2 servings

INGREDIENTS

- 1 cup (150 g) fresh cherries, pitted
- 2 scoops (120 g) vanilla ice cream
- 1 cup (250 ml) cold milk
- 8 ice cubes
- Whipped cream, to serve
- Cherry syrup, to serve
- Chocolate syrup, to serve

METHOD

- In a blender, combine the cherries, ice cream, milk, and ice cubes. Blend until smooth.
- Pour into 2 chilled glasses. Serve topped with whipped cream. Drizzle with some cherry syrup and chocolate syrup.
- Enjoy.

NUTRITIONAL INFORMATION

Energy	Fat	Carbohydrates	Protein	Sodium
339 calories	14.3 g	46.1 g	7.8 g	126 mg

BANANA AVOCADO FRAPPE

Preparation Time	Total Time	Yield
5 minutes	5 minutes	2 servings

INGREDIENTS

- 1 (180 g) frozen banana, cut into small pieces
- 1/4 medium (50 g) avocado, cut into small pieces
- 1/2 cup (125 g) plain low-fat yogurt
- 1 cup (250 ml) cold milk
- 1 tablespoon (20 ml) honey
- 10 ice cubes
- Whipped cream, to serve

METHOD

- Combine the banana, avocado, yogurt, milk, honey, and ice cubes in a blender. Blend to desired consistency.
- Pour into 2 chilled glasses. Serve topped with some whipped cream.
- Enjoy.

NUTRITIONAL INFORMATION

Energy	Fat	Carbohydrates	Protein	Sodium
284 calories	13.0 g	35.0 g	9.0 g	112 mg

LYCHEE AND COCONUT FRAPPE

Preparation Time	Total Time	Yield
5 minutes	5 minutes	2 servings

INGREDIENTS

- 1 1/2 cup (285 g) lychees, pitted
- 1/4 cup (60 ml) coconut cream
- 2 tablespoons (40 ml) agave nectar
- 1 cup (250 ml) skim milk
- 12 ice cubes
- Fresh mint sprigs, for garnish
- Pitted lychees, for garnish

METHOD

- In a blender, combine the lychees, coconut cream, agave nectar, milk, and ice cubes. Blend until smooth.
- Pour into 2 chilled glasses. Garnish with lychees and mint sprigs.
- Serve and enjoy.

NUTRITIONAL INFORMATION

Energy	Fat	Carbohydrates	Protein	Sodium
272 calories	7.8 g	48.5 g	5.9 g	75 mg

APPLE GREEN TEA FRAPPE

Preparation Time	Total Time	Yield
5 minutes	5 minutes	2 servings

INGREDIENTS

- 1 cup (250 g) apple puree
- 1 tablespoon (7 g) green tea powder, plus more for garnish
- 2 tablespoons (40 ml) honey
- 1/4 teaspoon (1.5 ml) vanilla extract
- 1 cup (250 ml) almond milk
- 12 ice cubes
- Whipped cream, to serve

METHOD

- Place the apple puree, green tea powder, honey, vanilla extract, almond milk in a blender. Pulse a few times to dissolve the green tea powder.
- Add the ice cubes and blend the mixture again until smooth.
- Pour into 2 chilled glasses. Serve topped with whipped cream and sprinkle with some green tea powder.
- Serve and enjoy.

NUTRITIONAL INFORMATION

Energy	Fat	Carbohydrates	Protein	Sodium
175 calories	6.0 g	31.4 g	31.4 g	84 mg

TUTTI FRUTTI FRAPPE

Preparation Time	Total Time	Yield
5 minutes	5 minutes	2 servings

INGREDIENTS

- 2 scoops (120 g) vanilla ice cream
- 1/2 cup (125 ml) milk
- 1/2 cup (125 g) plain yogurt
- 2 tablespoons (30 ml) bubble gum flavored syrup
- 12 ice cubes
- Whipped cream, to serve

METHOD

- Combine the vanilla ice cream, milk, yogurt, syrup, and ice cubes in a blender. Process until smooth.
- Pour into 2 chilled glasses. Serve topped with some whipped cream and candy sprinkles.
- Enjoy.

NUTRITIONAL INFORMATION

Energy	Fat	Carbohydrates	Protein	Sodium
284 calories	10.8 g	39.0 g	8.0 g	125 mg

MANGO BANANA AND ALMOND FRAPPE

Preparation Time	Total Time	Yield
5 minutes	5 minutes	2 servings

INGREDIENTS

- 1 cup (165 g) mango, cut into small pieces
- 1 (180 g) frozen banana, cut into small pieces
- 1 cup (250 ml) almond milk
- 10 ice cubes
- Chopped almonds, to serve

METHOD

- Blend all of the ingredients together in a blender to a smooth consistency.
- Pour into 2 chilled glasses. Top with some chopped almonds.
- Serve immediately and enjoy.

NUTRITIONAL INFORMATION

Energy	Fat	Carbohydrates	Protein	Sodium
202 calories	5.1 g	40.3 g	3.8 g	81 mg

KIWI COCONUT AND PINEAPPLE FRAPPE

Preparation Time	Total Time	Yield
5 minutes	5 minutes	2 servings

INGREDIENTS

- 2 (85 g) kiwi, cut into small pieces
- 1 cup (250 g) pineapple, cut into small pieces
- 1/4 cup (60 ml) coconut milk
- 1/4 teaspoon (1.5 ml) vanilla extract
- 1 tablespoon (20 ml) agave nectar or honey
- 1 cup (250 ml) coconut water
- 10 ice cubes

METHOD

- Combine kiwi, pineapple, coconut milk, vanilla extract, agave nectar, coconut water, and ice cubes in a blender; blend until smooth.
- Pour into 2 chilled glasses. Garnish with some kiwi slices and mint sprigs, if desired.
- Serve immediately and enjoy.

NUTRITIONAL INFORMATION

Energy	Fat	Carbohydrates	Protein	Sodium
224 calories	8.1 g	39.4 g	3.2 g	132 mg

BANANA RASPBERRY YOGURT FRAPPE

Preparation Time	Total Time	Yield
5 minutes	5 minutes	2 servings

INGREDIENTS

- 1 cup (220 g) frozen raspberries
- 1 (180 g) frozen banana, cut into small pieces
- 1 cup (250 g) plain Greek yogurt
- 1/2 cup (125 ml) almond milk
- 8 ice cubes
- Banana slices, for garnish
- Raspberries, for garnish
- Fresh mint sprig, for garnish

METHOD

- Put the raspberries, banana, yogurt, almond milk, and ice cubes in a blender. Blend until smooth and then pour into 2 chilled glasses.
- Garnish with banana slices, raspberries, and mint sprig.
- Serve immediately and enjoy.

NUTRITIONAL INFORMATION

Energy	Fat	Carbohydrates	Protein	Sodium
214 calories	3.9 g	33.3 g	14.6 g	80 mg

STRAWBERRY BANANA AND YOGURT FRAPPE

Preparation Time	Total Time	Yield
5 minutes	5 minutes	2 servings

INGREDIENTS

- 1 cup (220 g) frozen strawberries, hulled and halved
- 1 (180 g) frozen banana, cut into small pieces
- 1 cup (250 g) plain Greek yogurt
- 1/2 cup (125 ml) cold milk
- 8 ice cubes
- Strawberry halves, for garnish
- Fresh mint sprig, for garnish

METHOD

- Put the strawberries, banana, yogurt, cold milk, and ice cubes in a blender. Blend them together nicely and then pour into 2 chilled glasses.
- Garnish with strawberry halves and mint sprigs.
- Serve immediately and enjoy.

NUTRITIONAL INFORMATION

Energy	Fat	Carbohydrates	Protein	Sodium
247 calories	3.5 g	44.3 g	12.8 g	67 mg

FRUITY BLAST FRAPPE

Preparation Time	Total Time	Yield
5 minutes	5 minutes	4 servings

INGREDIENTS

- 1 cup (220 g) frozen strawberries
- 1 (180 g) frozen banana, sliced
- 1 cup (165 g) peaches, diced
- 4 scoops (240 g) vanilla ice cream
- 1 cup (250 ml) cold milk
- 12 ice cubes

METHOD

- Place the strawberries, banana, peaches, and ice cream in a high-speed blender. Blend until smooth.
- Add ice cubes and milk; blend again until smooth.
- Pour into 4 chilled glasses.
- Serve immediately.

NUTRITIONAL INFORMATION

Energy	Fat	Carbohydrates	Protein	Sodium
247 calories	3.5 g	44.3 g	12.8 g	67 mg

ULTIMATE CHOCOLATE FRAPPE

Preparation Time	Total Time	Yield
5 minutes	5 minutes	2 servings

INGREDIENTS

- 4 scoops (240 g) chocolate ice cream
- 1 cup (250 ml) cold milk
- 2 tablespoons (40 ml) chocolate syrup
- 8 ice cubes

METHOD

- Put the chocolate ice cream in a blender along with the milk, chocolate syrup, and ice cubes; blend until smooth.
- Pour into 2 glasses and enjoy. Drizzle with chocolate syrup if desired.
- Serve and enjoy.

NUTRITIONAL INFORMATION

Energy	Fat	Carbohydrates	Protein	Sodium
278 calories	11.1 g	37.4 g	7.2 g	135 mg

CHOCO LOCO FRAPPE

Preparation Time	Total Time	Yield
5 minutes	5 minutes	2 servings

INGREDIENTS

- 1 cup (250 ml) cold milk
- 4 scoops (250 g) chocolate ice cream
- 2 tablespoons (40 ml) dark chocolate syrup
- 4 tablespoons (60 g) powdered chocolate drink mix
- 6 ice cubes
- Chocolate-coated wafer bar, cut into cubes

METHOD

- In a blender, combine the cold milk, chocolate ice cream, dark chocolate syrup, powdered chocolate, and ice cubes. Blend until smooth.
- Pour into 2 glasses. Serve topped with some whipped cream and 2 chocolate-coated wafer cubes.
- Enjoy.

NUTRITIONAL INFORMATION

Energy	Fat	Carbohydrates	Protein	Sodium
247 calories	3.5 g	44.3 g	12.8 g	67 mg

COOKIE CRUMBLE FRAPPE

Preparation Time	Total Time	Yield
5 minutes	5 minutes	2 servings

INGREDIENTS

- 4 scoops (240 g) vanilla ice cream
- 1 cup (250 ml) almond milk, unsweetened
- 1 teaspoon (5 ml) pure vanilla extract
- 4 chocolate sandwich cookies (such as Oreo), crushed
- 4-6 ice cubes
- Whipped cream, to serve

METHOD

- Combine the ice cream, almond milk, vanilla extract, chocolate sandwich cookies, and ice cubes in a blender until smooth.
- Pour into 2 chilled glasses and top with some whipped cream.
- Serve immediately and enjoy.

NUTRITIONAL INFORMATION

Energy	Fat	Carbohydrates	Protein	Sodium
247 calories	3.5 g	44.3 g	12.8 g	67 mg

AVOCADO MATCHA FRAPPE

Preparation Time	Total Time	Yield
5 minutes	5 minutes	2 servings

INGREDIENTS

- 1 (200 g) avocado, diced
- 4 tablespoons (60 g) sweetened condensed milk
- 2 tablespoon (30 g) dry milk powder
- 1 tablespoon matcha powder
- 1 cup (250 ml) almond milk, unsweetened
- 10 ice cubes
- Whipped cream, to serve
- Matcha powder, to serve

METHOD

- In a blender, combine the avocado, sweetened condensed milk, powdered milk, matcha powder, almond milk, and ice cubes. Blend until smooth.
- Pour into 2 chilled glasses. Top with some whipped cream and sprinkle with matcha powder.
- Serve and enjoy.

NUTRITIONAL INFORMATION

Energy	Fat	Carbohydrates	Protein	Sodium
247 calories	3.5 g	44.3 g	12.8 g	67 mg

CINNAMON-SPICED APPLE FRAPPE

Preparation Time	Total Time	Yield
5 minutes	5 minutes	2 servings

INGREDIENTS

- 1 (180 g) apple, peeled, cored, and chopped
- 1 cup (250 ml) almond milk, unsweetened
- 2 scoops (120 g) vanilla ice cream
- 2 tablespoons (30 ml) sweetened condensed milk
- 1 teaspoon (2 g) ground cinnamon, plus more for garnish
- 10 ice cubes

METHOD

- Combine the apple, almond milk, vanilla ice cream, sweetened condensed milk, and cinnamon in a blender. Blend until smooth.
- Pour into 2 chilled glasses. Sprinkle a dash of cinnamon powder.
- Serve immediately and enjoy.

NUTRITIONAL INFORMATION

Energy	Fat	Carbohydrates	Protein	Sodium
266 calories	7.5 g	49.1 g	4.0 g	133 mg

ORANGE PEACH SOY FRAPPE

Preparation Time	Total Time	Yield
5 minutes	5 minutes	2 servings

INGREDIENTS

- 1 cup (150 g) peaches, diced
- 4 scoops (240 g) vanilla ice cream
- 1 1/2 cups (375 ml) soy milk
- 1/4 cup (60 ml) orange juice
- 8 ice cubes
- Orange slices, for garnish
- Mint sprigs, for garnish

METHOD

- In a blender, combine the peaches, vanilla ice cream, soy milk, orange juice, and ice cubes. Blend until smooth.
- Pour into 2 chilled glasses. Garnish frappe with orange slices and mint sprigs.
- Serve and enjoy.

NUTRITIONAL INFORMATION

Energy	Fat	Carbohydrates	Protein	Sodium
247 calories	3.5 g	44.3 g	12.8 g	67 mg

MANGO VANILLA FRAPPE

Preparation Time	Total Time	Yield
5 minutes	5 minutes	2 servings

INGREDIENTS

- 1 cup (165 g) mangoes, diced
- 1 (180 g) frozen banana, sliced
- 1 scoop (60 g) vanilla ice cream
- 1/4 teaspoon (0.5 g) ground cinnamon
- 1/4 teaspoon (0.5 g) ground nutmeg
- 1 cup (250 ml) almond milk
- 10 ice cubes

METHOD

- Put the mangoes, banana, ice cream, cinnamon, nutmeg, almond milk, and ice cubes in a blender. Blend them together until smooth.
- Pour into 2 chilled glasses. Garnish with a few diced mangoes.
- Serve immediately and enjoy.

NUTRITIONAL INFORMATION

Energy	Fat	Carbohydrates	Protein	Sodium
247 calories	3.5 g	44.3 g	12.8 g	67 mg

MALTED CHOCO AND BANANA FRAPPE

Preparation Time	Total Time	Yield
5 minutes	5 minutes	2 servings

INGREDIENTS

- 1 (150 g) frozen banana, cut into small pieces
- 6 tablespoons (50 g) powdered chocolate-flavored malt drink mix
- 1 cup (250 ml) almond milk
- 4 scoops (240 g) vanilla ice cream
- 6 ice cubes
- Chocolate syrup, to serve
- Whipped cream, to serve

METHOD

- Combine the frozen banana, powdered chocolate malt drink, almond milk, vanilla ice cream, and ice cubes in a blender. Blend until smooth and creamy.
- Drizzle the sides of 2 chilled glasses with chocolate syrup. Pour the frappe and top with some whipped cream.
- Serve immediately and enjoy.

NUTRITIONAL INFORMATION

Energy	Fat	Carbohydrates	Protein	Sodium
247 calories	3.5 g	44.3 g	12.8 g	67 mg

STRAWBERRY KIWI FRAPPE

Preparation Time	Total Time	Yield
5 minutes	5 minutes	2 servings

INGREDIENTS

- 1 cup (220 g) frozen strawberries
- 1 medium (85 g) kiwifruit, diced
- 1 cup (250 ml) cold milk
- 2 scoops (120 g) vanilla ice cream
- 6 ice cubes
- Whipped cream, to serve
- Strawberries, for garnish

METHOD

- Place the strawberries, kiwi, cold milk, vanilla ice cream, and ice cubes in a high-speed blender. Blend until smooth.
- Pour into 2 chilled glasses. Top with some whipped cream and garnish with strawberries.
- Serve immediately and enjoy.

NUTRITIONAL INFORMATION

Energy	Fat	Carbohydrates	Protein	Sodium
247 calories	3.5 g	44.3 g	12.8 g	67 mg

WATERMELON BANANA YOGURT FRAPPE

Preparation Time	Total Time	Yield
5 minutes	5 minutes	2 servings

INGREDIENTS

- 2 cups (300 g) watermelon, cubed
- 1 (180 g) frozen banana, sliced
- 3/4 cup (185 g) plain yogurt
- 8 ice cubes
- Fresh mint sprigs, for garnish

METHOD

- Process the watermelon, banana, yogurt, and ice cubes in a blender until smooth.
- Pour into 2 chilled glasses. Garnish with mint sprigs.
- Serve immediately and enjoy.

NUTRITIONAL INFORMATION

Energy	Fat	Carbohydrates	Protein	Sodium
247 calories	3.5 g	44.3 g	12.8 g	67 mg

THICK CHOCOLATE FRAPPE WITH MALLOWS

Preparation Time	Total Time	Yield
5 minutes	5 minutes	2 servings

INGREDIENTS

- 2 scoops (120 g) vanilla ice cream
- 2 scoops (120 g) chocolate ice cream
- 1 cup (250 g) almond milk
- 1/4 cup (40 g) powdered chocolate drink mix
- 6 ice cubes
- Marshmallows, to serve

METHOD

- In a blender, combine the vanilla and chocolate ice cream, almond milk, powdered chocolate drink mix, and ice cubes. Cover, and blend until smooth.
- Pour into 2 chilled glasses. Top with some marshmallows.
- Serve immediately and enjoy.

NUTRITIONAL INFORMATION

Energy	Fat	Carbohydrates	Protein	Sodium
247 calories	3.5 g	44.3 g	12.8 g	67 mg

MOCHA CHEESECAKE FRAPPE

Preparation Time	Total Time	Yield
5 minutes	5 minutes	2 servings

INGREDIENTS

- 1 cup (250 ml) cooled, strong brewed coffee
- 1/2 cup (125 g) cream cheese
- 1/2 cup (125 ml) skim milk
- 2 tablespoons (40 ml) sweetened condensed milk
- 1 tablespoon (7 g) unsweetened cocoa powder
- 1/4 teaspoon (1.5 ml) vanilla extract
- 12 ice cubes
- Whipped cream, to serve
- Chocolate syrup, to serve

METHOD

- In a blender, combine the coffee, cream cheese, skim milk, condensed milk, cocoa powder, vanilla extract, and ice cubes. Blend until smooth.
- Pour into 2 chilled glasses. Top with some whipped cream and drizzle with chocolate syrup.
- Serve immediately and enjoy.

NUTRITIONAL INFORMATION

Energy	Fat	Carbohydrates	Protein	Sodium
247 calories	3.5 g	44.3 g	12.8 g	67 mg

BLUEBERRY BANANA FRAPPE

Preparation Time	Total Time	Yield
5 minutes	5 minutes	2 servings

INGREDIENTS

- 1 cup (250 ml) skim milk
- 2 scoops (120 g) vanilla ice cream
- 1 cup (155 g) frozen blueberries
- 1 (180 g) frozen banana, sliced
- 1/4 teaspoon (1.5 ml) vanilla extract
- 6 ice cubes

METHOD

- Combine the milk, vanilla ice cream, blueberries, banana, vanilla extract, and ice cubes in a blender. Blend until smooth.
- Pour into 2 chilled glasses. Garnish with blueberries if desired.
- Serve immediately and enjoy.

NUTRITIONAL INFORMATION

Energy	Fat	Carbohydrates	Protein	Sodium
247 calories	3.5 g	44.3 g	12.8 g	67 mg

RECIPE INDEX

A

Almond Caramel Coffee Frappe 30
Almond Chocolate Frappe 23
Almond Peach Frappe 37
Amaretto Coffee Frappe 32
Apple Green Tea Frappe 47
Arabica Coffee and Nutella Frappe 33
Avocado Matcha Frappe 57

B

Banana Avocado Frappe 45
Banana Raspberry Yogurt Frappe 51
Banana Split Frappe 2
Black Forest Frappe 43
Blueberry Banana Frappe 66

C

Caramel Mocha Frappe 40
Cherry Frappe Blast 18
Cherry Vanilla Frappe 44
Choco Banana Frappe 25
Chocolate Hazelnut Frappe 5
Chocolate Raspberry Frappe 16
Chocolate Ricotta Frappe 21
Choco Loco Frappe 55
Choco Strawberry and Coconut Frappe 7
Cinnamon-Spiced Apple Frappe 58
Cinnamon-Spiced Coffee Frappe 3
Coffee Caramel Apple Frappe 19
Coffee Crumble Frappe 31
Coffee Peanut Butter Frappe 20
Cookie Crumble Frappe 56
Cookies and Cream Frappe 9

D

Dark Mocha Frappe 10
Decadent Tiramisu Frappe 11

Deep Dark Chocolate Frappe 24

F

Fruity Blast Frappe 53

H

Horchata Frappe 13

K

Kiwi Coconut and Pineapple Frappe 50

L

Lychee and Coconut Frappe 46

M

Macadamia Chocolate Frappe 38
Malted Choco and Banana Frappe 61
Mango Banana and Almond Frappe 49
Mango Vanilla Frappe 60
Mexican Chocolate Frappe 14
Minty Mocha Frappe 41
Mocha Cheesecake Frappe 65
Mocha Java Frappe 26

O

Orange Peach Soy Frappe 59

P

Peppermint Mocha Frappe 22
Pumpkin Caramel Frappe 35

R

Rich Chocolate Frappe 4

S

Soy Chocolate Frappe 8
Spiced Mocha Frappe 36
Spiced Pumpkin and Caramel Frappe 15

Strawberry and White Chocolate Frappe 29
Strawberry Banana and Yogurt Frappe 52
Strawberry Kiwi Frappe 62
Strawberry Vanilla Frappe 39
Sugar-Free Green Tea Frappe 12

T

Thick Chocolate Frappe with Mallows 64
Tutti Frutti Frappe 48

U

Ultimate Chocolate and Hazelnut Frappe 28
Ultimate Chocolate Frappe 54
Ultimate Mocha Frappe 6

W

Watermelon Banana Yogurt Frappe 63
White Chocolate and Caramel Frappe 27
White Chocolate Frappe 17
White Coffee Frappe 34
White Mocha Frappe 42

We want to thank you for purchasing this book. Our writers and creative team took pride in creating this book, and we have tried to make it as enjoyable as possible.

We would love to hear from you. Kindly leave us a review if you enjoyed this book so we can do more. Your reviews on our books are highly appreciated. Also, if you have any comments or suggestions, you may reach us at info@contentarcade.com

**Regards,
Content Arcade Publishing Team**

Made in the USA
Columbia, SC
28 December 2021